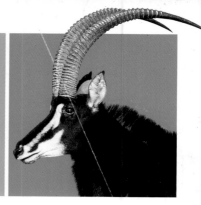

a first book of

animals

Christiane Gunzi

picthall and gunzi

Created and produced by
Picthall & Gunzi Limited
21A Widmore Road
Bromley BR1 1RW
United Kingdom

Copyright © 2011 Picthall & Gunzi Limited
First published in Great Britain as *My World Animals Discovering the Animal World* by Picthall and Gunzi Limited 2004

Editor: Christiane Gunzi
Designer: Dominic Zwemmer

Design assistance: Paul Calver & Ray Bryant
Editorial assistance: Carmen Hansen
Educational consultants: Diana Bentley, MA Advanced Diploma in Children's Literature, & Jane Whitwell, Diploma in Special Educational Needs
Natural history consultant: Barbara Taylor Cork

ISBN **978-1-907604-12-6**

Reproduction by Colourscan in Singapore
Printed and bound by WKT Company Ltd, China

For Bruce Coleman Limited:
Animal Ark, Franco Banfi, Erik Bjurstrom, Jane Burton, John Cancalosi, Alain Compost, Sarah Cook, Mike Hill, Harald Lange, Robert Maier, Joe McDonald, Natural Selection Inc, Dr Scott Nielsen, Pacific Stock, Photobank Yokohama, Andrew Purcell, Hans Reinhard, Kim Taylor, Colin Varndell, Jim Watt, Staffan Widstrand

For Frank Lane Picture Agency:
K Aitken/Panda, Ron Austing, F Bavendam/Minden, Richard Becker, J Brandenburg/Minden, B B Casals, Peter Davey, K Delport, Dembinsky, Wendy Dennis, Tom & Pam Gardner, J Hawkins, David Hosking, D & E Hosking, M Iwago/Minden, Gerard Lacz, F Lanting/Minden, T Mangelsen/Minden, K Maslowski, S Maslowski, Chris Mattison, W Meinderts/Foto Natura, M Moltett/Minden, Fritz Polking, C Rhodes, Walther Rohdich, L Lee Rue, Silvestris, Jurgen & Christine Sohns, M J Thomas, Roger Tidman, Larry West, T Whittaker, Roger Wilmshurst, D P Wilson, Winfried Wisniewski, Martin B Withers, K Wothe/Minden, S Yoshino/Minden

For ImageState:
Nick Garbutt, Martin Ruegner

For NHPA:
Daryl Balfour, Andy Rouse

For Science Photo Library:
Suzanne L & Joseph T Collins, Tim Davis

For Warren Photographic:
Jane Burton, Kim Taylor, Mark Taylor

For Woodfall Wild Images:
Adrian Dorst

Please note that every effort has been made to check the accuracy of the information contained in this book, and to credit the copyright holders correctly. Picthall & Gunzi apologize for any unintentional errors or omissions, and would be happy to include revisions to content and/or acknowledgements in subsequent editions of this book.

Contents

All the main groups of animals are presented here in a clear and simple way, including mammals, birds, reptiles, amphibians, fish and insects.

From beetles and butterflies to ants and bees, all the best-known insects are shown here, along with spiders and scorpions. Youngsters are encouraged to find and count all the different groups of mini-beasts.

Here children are introduced to the fascinating world of fish, from huge whale sharks to little sticklebacks and seahorses. Questions encourage children to recognize and learn the colours, shapes and sizes of fish too.

Children discover a variety of different mammals and learn that they are usually covered in fur (or hair), and range in size from the velvety mole to the hairy bison.

Birds from all over the world are shown, from the tiny sparrow to the huge ostrich. Questions help children to understand that birds have beaks, most birds can fly, and many birds have babies in nests.

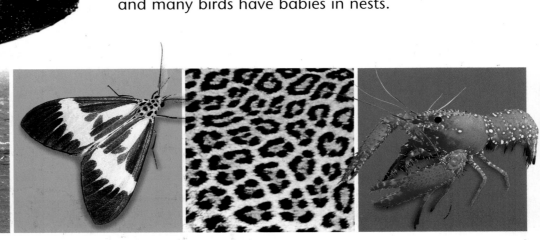

Notes to parents & caregivers

This book was created with the help of educational experts and parents to provide young children with an exciting introduction to the world of animals. With the help of stimulating questions and activities throughout the book, *A First Book of Animals* covers all the main animal groups in a straightforward and systematic manner. Entertaining and educational, it also builds essential pre-school skills in the areas of number recognition and language development.

A shoal of bigeyes

Using this book and beyond...

- For information about the specific content of any of the pages, refer to the contents list at the front of this book.
- Work at your child's pace, and allow him or her to choose some of the pages to talk about.
- Encourage your child to show you, and talk about, any animals in the book that particularly interest him or her.
- When you are out and about, point out any animals you see, and encourage your child to talk about these too.

Let's meet the animals!

A First Book of Animals has been structured so that children are introduced to animal groups one at a time. The book opens with an overview of all the main groups, including insects, birds, reptiles and fish. Then there are features on each group, from little mini-beasts to large mammals. Later on, children can take a look at animal homes, how animals move, animal camouflage and animal babies. Each wildlife topic is presented clearly and simply. There are over 200 colourful photographs of some of the world's best-known animals, along with a few less familiar ones.

Using this book

When looking at this book with your child, it is important to create a relaxed atmosphere, allowing the child to set his or her own pace. Encourage the child and give lots of praise, and always try to finish on a positive note.

By encouraging youngsters to make the vital connections between the words and pictures, you will help to build their confidence and encourage them to enjoy learning. As you work through the pages together, look beyond the book too, and talk about other wildlife topics that may interest your child.

Enjoy yourselves!

Remember, the most effective way for children to extend their understanding of the world around them is through play and enjoyment. However you choose to use this book, there are many hours of entertainment and learning to be shared. Above all, have fun!

Challenging interactive questions at the top of the pages will encourage children to look at the pictures more closely.

Specially-devised activities on each page will help to hold children's attention and keep them entertained.

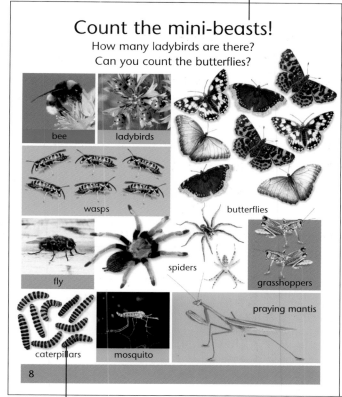

Count the mini-beasts!
How many ladybirds are there?
Can you count the butterflies?

bee ladybirds

wasps

butterflies

fly spiders

grasshoppers

praying mantis

caterpillars mosquito

8

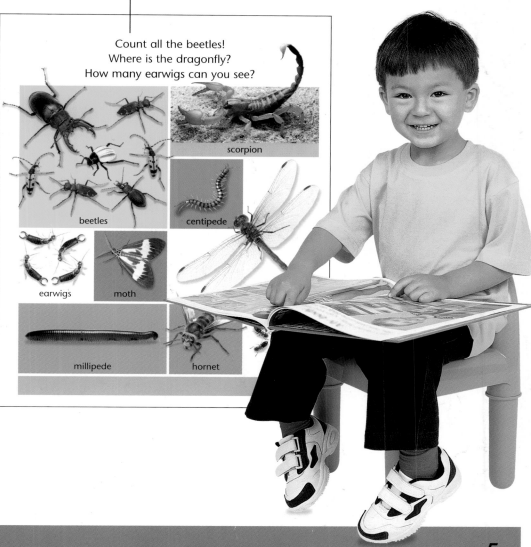

Count all the beetles!
Where is the dragonfly?
How many earwigs can you see?

scorpion

beetles centipede

earwigs moth

millipede hornet

Bright, colourful photographs of over 200 different animals engage children's interest.

Meet the animals!

Which animals have six legs?
Which animals are covered in feathers?

Slugs and worms are soft and slimy.

worms

slug

slugs and worms

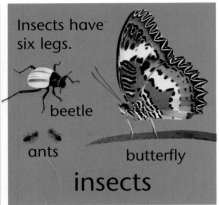

Insects have six legs.

beetle

ants

butterfly

insects

Spiders and scorpions have eight legs.

scorpion

spider

spiders and scorpions

Crabs and lobsters have hard shells.

crab

lobster

crabs and lobsters

Frogs and toads live on land and in water.

frog

toad

frogs and toads

Snakes and tortoises are called reptiles. Reptiles have scaly skin.

snake

reptiles

tortoise

All birds have feathers and most birds can fly!

swallow

hummingbird

dove

macaw

puffin

heron

birds

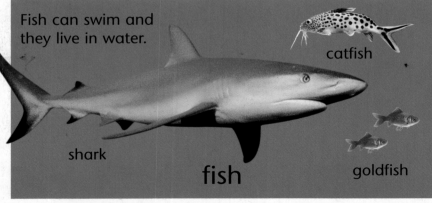

Fish can swim and they live in water.

catfish

shark

fish

goldfish

Which of these animals are furry?
Point to the little mouse!
Do you know the names of all the animals?

hippopotamus

chimpanzees

mouse

gerbil

monkey

All mammals feed their babies with milk, and some mammals are very furry!

anteater

rhinoceros

giraffe

whale

mammals

Count the mini-beasts!
How many ladybirds are there?
Can you count the butterflies?

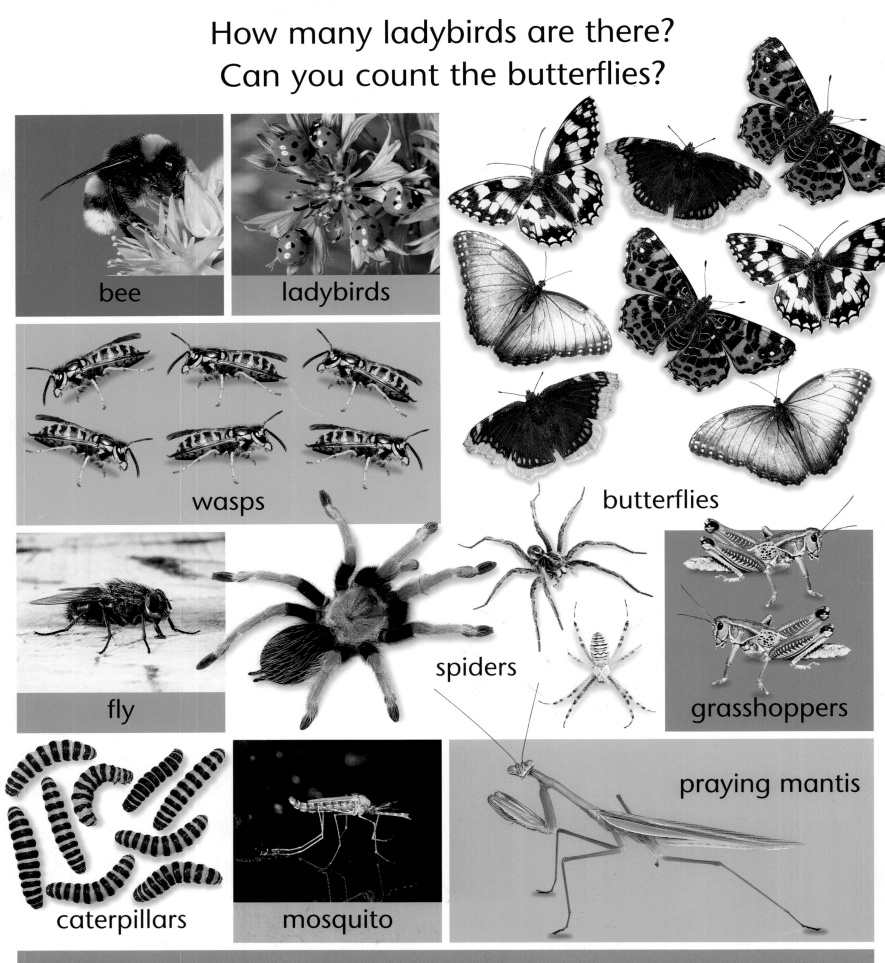

bee

ladybirds

wasps

butterflies

fly

spiders

grasshoppers

caterpillars

mosquito

praying mantis

Count all the beetles!
Where is the dragonfly?
How many earwigs can you see?

scorpion

beetles

centipede

earwigs

moth

dragonfly

millipede

hornet

ants

Super swimmers

Where is the shoal of orange fish?
Can you find the two sticklebacks?

butterfly fish

piranha fish

lionfish

cod

a shoal of bigeyes

sticklebacks

reef shark

Can you see the huge whale shark?
Point to the long swordfish!
Where is the yellow seahorse?

whale shark

swordfish

angelfish

snapper

seahorse

ray

Furry animals

Where is the furry black bear?
How many koalas can you see?

gorilla

squirrel

possum

lion

black bear

guinea pig

beaver

koalas

What is the panda doing?
Can you find the big, strong gorilla?
Point to the lion's furry mane!

mole

groundhog

camel

wolf

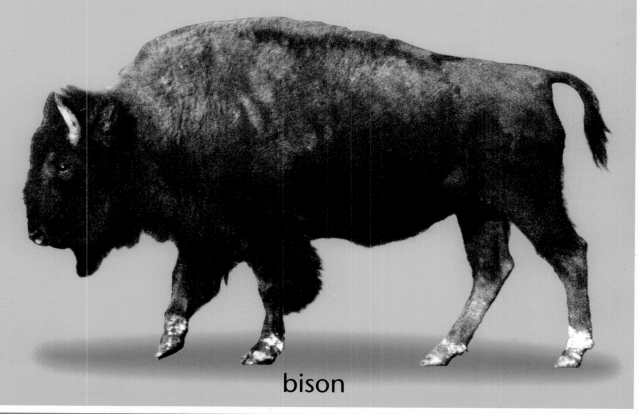

bison

panda

Feathers and wings
Which of these birds are flying?
Can you see the sparrow on a twig?

sparrow

swallow

pelican

penguin

eagle

pigeon

flamingo

goose

owl

vulture

emu

Can you find some baby birds in a nest?
Which bird has fish in its beak?
Point to the ostrich and the emu!

gull

parrot

kestrel

thrush

woodpecker

puffin

ostrich

Scaly animals
Which animal is swimming in the sea?
Can you find the three snakes?

alligator

cobra

chameleon

turtle

viper

komodo dragon

Which scaly animal has lots of sharp teeth?
Can you see the little green gecko?
Where is the chameleon with the curly tail?

boa

iguana

tortoise

skink

gecko

lizard

crocodile

Frogs and their family

Where is the green frog with red eyes?
Can you count the tadpoles?

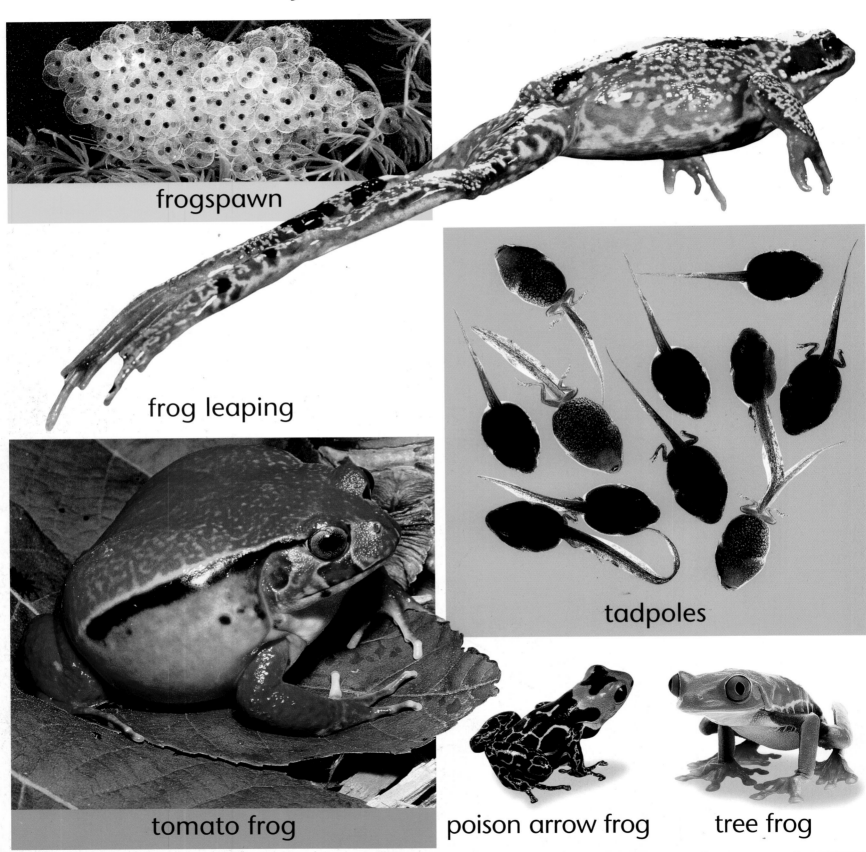

frogspawn

frog leaping

tadpoles

tomato frog

poison arrow frog

tree frog

Can you find the toad with bumpy skin?
Which animals are swimming?
Point to the salamander!

common frog

newt

axolotl

salamander

toad

Run, jump, leap and fly!
Can you see the owl flying?
What is the gibbon doing?

owl flying

lion
running

gibbon swinging

snail
crawling

octopus
swimming

impala leaping

Which birds are diving into the sea?
Can you find the raccoon climbing a tree?
What is the cheetah doing?

kangaroo hopping

dolphin jumping

penguins diving

raccoon climbing

cheetah racing

snake slithering

wildebeest walking

Eyes, ears and big teeth!

Point to the animals with big ears!
Which animals have long tusks?

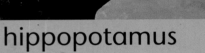
hippopotamus

bobcat

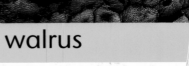
walrus

shark

Can you find some animals with whiskers?
Where is the fish with very sharp teeth?
Point to the animal with its tongue out!

toucan

bushbaby

komodo dragon

fennec fox

elephant

Horns, antlers, spines and shells

Can you see the crab with a hard shell?
Which animal has a big horn on its nose?

crab

armadillo

rhinoceros

porcupine fish

moose

Which two animals have antlers?
Can you find the armadillo?
Point to the animals with spines!

sea urchin

porcupine

buffalo

caribou

hedgehog

antelope

Spots and stripes
Point to the spotted leopard!
Can you find another spotted animal?

leopard

chipmunk

frog

caiman

diver

eel

dalmatians

Where is the stripy tiger?
How many stripy animals can you find?
Say the names of all the animals!

ladybirds

zebra

lemurs

gecko

butterfly

tiger

triggerfish

What animals do
Which of these animals are eating?
Point to the animals that are sleeping!

rabbit yawning

bee carrying

lioness washing

orang utan playing

otter sleeping

tortoise eating

Which two animals are playing?
Find the animals that are carrying something!
Can you see the jaguar drinking?

kingfisher carrying

arctic fox sleeping

fish hiding

koala eating

puppy playing

jaguar drinking

Animals and their babies

Where is the cat with a fluffy kitten?
Can you see the horse and foal?

dog and puppies

swan and cygnets

goat and kid

cat and kitten

deer and fawn

horse and foal

fox and cub

elephant and
elephant calf

How many bear cubs are there?
Point to the pig and piglets!
Can you count all the ducklings?

hen and chicks

sheep and lamb

pig and piglets

bear and cubs

cow and calf

kangaroo and joey

duck and ducklings

seal and pup

Where animals live

Which animals live in the snow?
Where do whales live?

tiger in the forest

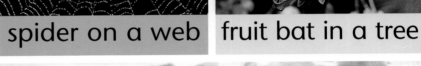

spider on a web

fruit bat in a tree

polar bears in the snow

mouse in a hole

starfish in a pool

whale in the ocean

rabbit in a burrow